Gaenslen

21st Century
Basic Skills
Library

HOW'S THE WEATHER IN FALL?

by Rebecca Felix

Cherry Lake Publishing • Ann Arbor, Michigan

1

Published in the United States of America
by Cherry Lake Publishing
Ann Arbor, Michigan
www.cherrylakepublishing.com

Consultant: Marla Conn, Read-Ability

Photo Credits: Brykaylo Yuriy/Shutterstock Images, cover, 1; Vibrant Image Studio/Shutterstock Images, 4; Jaren Jai Wicklund/Shutterstock Images, 6, 16; Shutterstock Images, 8; Jason Taylor/iStockphoto, 10; Dave Allen Photography/Shutterstock Images, 12; George Bailey/iStockphoto, 14; Kyu Oh/iStockphoto, 18; Alexander Semenov/iStockphoto, 20

Library of Congress Cataloging-in-Publication Data
Felix, Rebecca, 1984-
  How's the weather in fall? / Rebecca Felix
     p. cm. -- (Let's look at fall)
  Includes index.
  Audience: 005-007.
  Audience: K-3.
  ISBN 978-1-61080-902-3 (hardback : alk. paper) -- ISBN 978-1-61080-927-6 (paperback : alk. paper) -- ISBN 978-1-61080-952-8 (ebook) -- ISBN 978-1-61080-977-1 (hosted ebook)
  1. Autumn--Juvenile literature. 2. Weather--Juvenile literature. 3. Weather forecasting--Juvenile literature. I. Title. II. Series: Felix, Rebecca, 1984- Let's look at fall.

QB637.7.F445 2013
551.6--dc23

                          2012030453

Cherry Lake Publishing would like to acknowledge
the work of The Partnership for 21st Century Skills.
Please visit www.21stcenturyskills.org for more information.

Printed in the United States of America
Corporate Graphics Inc.
January 2013
CLFA10

TABLE OF CONTENTS

5 **Fall Season**

9 **Cold**

15 **Wind**

19 **Sunlight**

22 Find Out More

22 Glossary

23 Home and School Connection

23 What Do You See?

24 Index

24 About the Author

Fall Season

Fall is a season. It brings many changes.

Tess sees leaves change color. The **temperature** changes, too.

What Do You See?

What colors are Luke's hat?

8

Cold

Luke feels it is colder. He wears warmer clothes.

Animals sense cold weather, too. Squirrels gather food to **prepare** for winter.

Winter is too cold for most leaves. They change color and fall.

What Do You See?

What color leaves do you see?

Wind

Chilly winds blow in fall. Fallen leaves **float** in the wind.

Fall weather is **crisp**. Claire feels the cool, clear air.

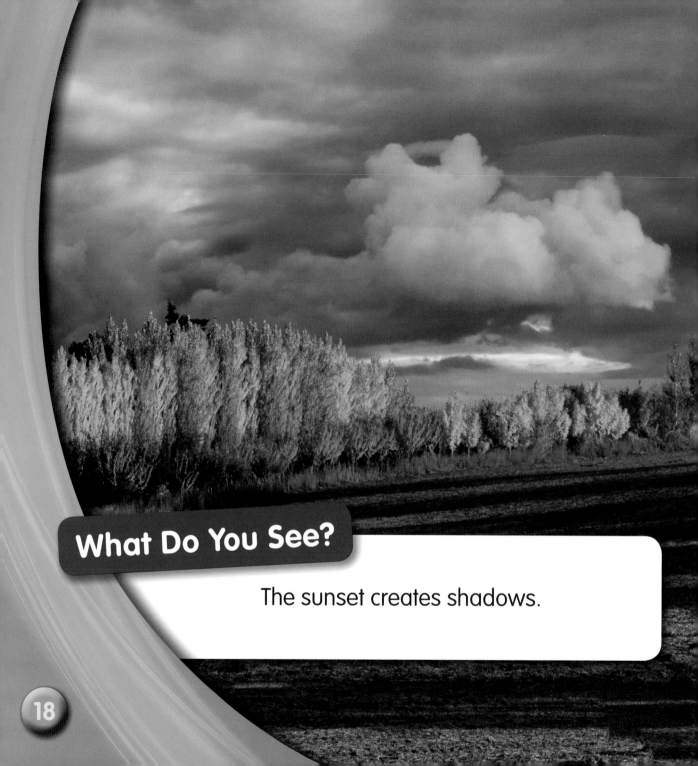

What Do You See?

The sunset creates shadows.

18

Sunlight

The sun goes down earlier in fall. Days get shorter.

Longer nights grow cold. Drew sees snow. Winter is on the way!

Find Out More

BOOK

Frank, John. *A Chill in the Air: Nature Poems for Fall and Winter*. New York: Simon & Schuster, 2003.

WEB SITE

The Weather Channel Kids!
www.theweatherchannelkids.com
Find information and games about the different seasons.

Glossary

crisp (KRISP) weather that is cool and clear

float (FLOHT) moving lightly and slowly through air or water

prepare (prih-PAIR) to get ready

temperature (TEM-pur-uh-chur) how hot or cold something is

Home and School Connection

Use this list of words from the book to help your child become a better reader. Word games and writing activities can help beginning readers reinforce literacy skills.

air	crisp	longer	sunlight
animals	earlier	nights	sunset
blow	fall	prepare	temperature
change	fallen	season	warmer
chilly	feels	sense	wears
clear	float	shadows	weather
clothes	food	shorter	wind
cold	gather	snow	winter
color	hat	squirrels	
cool	leaves	sun	

What Do You See?

What Do You See? is a feature paired with select photos in this book. It encourages young readers to interact with visual images in order to build the ability to integrate content in various media formats.

You can help your child further evaluate photos in this book with additional activities. Look at the images in the book without the What Do You See? feature. Ask your child to point out one detail in each image, such as the time of day or setting.

Index

animals, 11

change, 5, 7, 13
chilly, 15
clothes, 9
cold, 9, 11, 13, 21
crisp, 17

leaves, 7, 13, 14, 15

snow, 21
sun, 18, 19

temperature, 7

wind, 15
winter, 11, 13, 21

About the Author

Rebecca Felix is an editor and writer from Minnesota. The weather there is crisp and cool in fall. Then winter arrives, and it gets very cold in Minnesota!